Difficult Conversations

20 MINUTE MANAGER SERIES

Get up to speed fast on essential business skills. Whether you're looking for a crash course or a brief refresher, you'll find just what you need in HBR's 20-Minute Manager series—foundational reading for ambitious professionals and aspiring executives. Each book is a concise, practical primer, so you'll have time to brush up on a variety of key management topics.

Advice you can quickly read and apply, from the most trusted source in business.

Titles include:

Creating Business Plans
Delegating Work
Difficult Conversations
Finance Basics
Getting Work Done
Giving Effective Feedback
Innovative Teams
Managing Projects
Managing Time
Managing Up
Performance Reviews
Presentations
Running Meetings

20 MINUTE MANAGER SERIES

Difficult Conversations

Craft a clear message
Manage emotions
Focus on a solution

HARVARD BUSINESS REVIEW PRESS

Boston, Massachusetts

Cataloging-in-Publication data is forthcoming

ISBN: 978-1-63369-078-3
eISBN: 978-1-63369-079-0

Preview

You've been putting off a difficult conversation. Maybe you feel wronged by someone or misunderstood. You may be caught in a clash of personalities or have competing goals with a colleague. Perhaps you have to deliver bad news, and you dread the person's reaction. Whatever your situation, you need to address an issue to keep moving forward. This book will help you develop the skills you need to turn a difficult conversation into a productive dialogue, including:

- Understanding what makes some conversations difficult

- Discovering what's at the heart of the challenge you're facing

- Identifying and managing the emotions involved

- Seeing the bigger picture to expand possible solutions

- Framing the issue in a way your counterpart can relate to

- Listening actively and responding with empathy

- Staying flexible and managing the unexpected

- Finding areas of agreement

- Building on your new skills so you'll be ready for the next tough conversation

Contents

Contents

Difficult Conversations

What Makes a Conversation Difficult?

What Makes a Conversation Difficult?

You know the feeling: that knot in the pit of your stomach; the fog that descends on your mind. You're avoiding a difficult conversation. Maybe you fear the public confrontation if you ask a colleague to stop interrupting you in meetings. Perhaps you don't know how to tell a fellow team member that she's not pulling her weight. Or you want to ask your boss for a promotion, but you don't know how to begin the discussion. Maybe you tried to bring up what you thought was a straightforward matter, but it fell flat. When you have a problem, people tell you to "talk about it," but no one tells you

3

how. This book will help you move from paralysis to productive action and find the right words and the right methods to express yourself.

At work we tend to focus on work: knocking off tasks, meeting our performance goals, getting a raise. But our inner lives—our personal goals, needs, aspirations, and fears—inform and influence everything we do. Both our functional agendas ("I need that production schedule by tomorrow!") and our emotional agendas ("The production manager's stonewalling made me look weak in the status meeting!") will sometimes collide with those of our coworkers. Misunderstandings, even conflicts, arise. Whether those disagreements throw us off balance and disrupt our work or lead to conversations that yield valuable insights and creative solutions is up to us.

A difficult conversation is one in which the other person has a viewpoint that differs from yours, one or both of you feel insecure in some way, and the stakes seem high. Whether you have tough feedback to deliver to an employee or colleague or whether you feel wronged, thwarted, or misunderstood by the other person, these situations can be unsettling, even if you're a pretty good communicator.

Understanding what's at the heart of your situation helps you conduct a more productive discussion. Let's look at some of the reasons why conversations are difficult.

Conflicting interests

Your role in the organization influences what you want to achieve in a situation. If, for example, you're a marketing manager on a major product update, your priority is probably hitting every rollout deadline. Your colleague in production, however, is focused on meeting design requirements. Of course, successfully delivering an important product requires meeting both quality and schedule specifications. But those differing interests will naturally cause conflict at times. You may find it tough to talk about them because each person quickly gets entrenched in their position ("We've got to improve call quality" versus "We have to cut costs by 5%"). Sometimes interests also become misaligned when outside-the-office needs, such as family commitments or health issues, conflict with those at work. Developing an awareness of the factors that affect each person's approach to the project in question allows us to find ways to accommodate them.

Different personal styles

You think of yourself as a doer—a no-nonsense person who just gets the job done. No intrigue, no drama. Your teammate is a talker. He asks lots of questions, thinks things through aloud, considers the unintended consequences. Usually your different styles are able to coexist—but there's a deadline looming, and the project feels bogged down. How do you get him to move from exploring possibilities to picking an approach and closing the deal?

Working closely with someone whose communication or work style, personality, values, or life experiences differ greatly from yours has the potential to spark creativity and innovation, but it can also lead to misunderstanding and tension. What seems like a self-evident conclusion to one person may not have even occurred to another.

The more you understand about your own personal style, the more you will become aware of how your counterpart's habits differ. Table 1, "Example of different work styles," shows how understanding your own and your colleague's traits helps you work together effectively despite your differences.

Later we'll look at how to use your understanding about personal style to decide whether to initiate a conversation and, if you do, to prepare and successfully conduct one. We're not suggesting that you'll be able to change your natural preferences or those of

TABLE 1

Example of different work styles

Trait	You	Your colleague
Personality type	You're an introvert. You keep to yourself and prefer to work independently.	He's an extrovert. He likes working in teams and discussing things in detail.
Communication style	You're uncomfortable expressing your feelings. You prefer e-mail to face-to-face communication.	He shares a lot and asks a lot of questions. He prefers informal meetings.
Work style	You're methodical. Details count.	He tends to think "big picture" and move quickly.
Life experience	You have years of experience—and battle scars.	He hasn't been on the job long, so he's trying to make a mark.
Core values	You care most about quality and integrity.	He cares most about innovation and action.

your counterpart. But if, say, you recognize that your extroverted colleague loves lively group discussions while you prefer to work independently, suggest that you take notes at a brainstorming session or send him a preliminary list of ideas to seed the conversation as a way for both of you to participate productively.

Lack of trust

Addressing a sensitive issue or working with someone on a contentious project is difficult, and it's likely to be even harder if you don't have a trusting relationship.

People's work styles often have an effect on their ability to build trust. If one person wants to carefully map out a detailed plan and the other wants to just get going on the project, it may be hard for them to connect. But small gestures of respect and concern for the other person's approach go a long way toward bridging differences.

There's more to trust than compatible personalities or work styles, though. We typically feel more trusting toward people with whom we share common interests and experiences. Positive past interactions, such as being on a team that delivered a successful project, can build trust. But if past interactions have been tough, or if your counterpart is in a position of relative power, you're more likely to be guarded. In addition, the specifics of your circumstance often dictate how trusting you feel (a board room presentation creates more formality and distance than a team lunch at a local café). And sometimes a situation just makes you feel vulnerable and thereby less likely to proactively address it.

Different views of the facts

Each of us has our own understanding of the facts. Our view is based on what we've experienced and observed from our unique, and limited, perspective.

If your job requires meeting weekly with a customer, your view of the essential facts of a project relate to deadlines made or missed. If your teammate is developing the product, her view of the essential facts relate to satisfying specifications or resolving bugs. You may well be unaware of what your counterpart's view of the "facts" consists of. Without shared information, you may both draw conclusions about the other's actions. Taking the time to think through your counterpart's perspectives will help prepare you for a difficult conversation.

Strong emotions

Your emotions are never far beneath the surface. Fear, anger, anxiety, and shame often underlie difficult conversations in the workplace. If you feel attacked, or if you feel that someone is trying to take advantage of you or sully your reputation, your natural response may be to fight back or to hide. Likewise, if you have to deliver bad news, such as a poor performance review or a missed deadline, you may warily anticipate the other person's strong reaction. This fight or flight response prevents you from stepping back and responding to the perceived threat in a calm way. But when we become aware of what we're feeling, we can start to manage those emotions. Likewise, when we think about how the other person's feelings affect how she responds, we're better equipped to take her feelings into account when proposing a productive way forward.

. . .

We've seen how varying interests, work styles, and views of the facts, as well as a lack of underlying trust, make it hard to communicate effectively. But the good news is that whether you're a new manager, a member of a mission-critical team, or an independent consultant, it's possible to make even a fraught relationship better through skillful communication. You'll alleviate the likelihood for duplicated efforts or working at cross-purposes. You'll be on the same page with your team and in front of your customers. You'll boost your self-confidence.

This book will be your guide. It will give you the tools to peel back and understand the complicated layers of difficult discussions and develop and practice the skills you need to manage them. In the next chapter, we'll look at when to have a tough conversation and how to discover opportunities amidst the challenges. In the middle of the book, we'll walk through the steps of shaping an effective conversation: thoroughly preparing for it, mindfully and adaptively conducting it—and, post-conversation, following through on next steps. Finally, we'll look at how to develop proactive communication skills to forge transparent, productive relationships going forward. Along the way we'll look at fictional examples of challenging interactions, assess what's actually going on, and explore how to shift the dynamic—and the outcome—by successfully navigating a difficult conversation.

Think It Through

Think It Through

Regardless of the factors that conspire to make an interaction difficult, it is possible to develop strategies and skills that will help. You may think that the problem originates with the other person, but successfully resolving it starts with you. You need to think about your situation differently.

In this chapter we'll focus on the introspective work you should do before involving the other person. This means honestly assessing whether the situation will benefit from a conversation and, if you determine it will, planning what steps you'll take to make the discussion productive.

Should you act?

Most of us would rather ignore a problem than confront it. Why risk a blowup or damage to the relationship— or to your reputation? Of course, if the problem you're facing isn't central to your success on the job, then it may make sense to leave it be. But if you're brooding about a dismissive remark a rival made or replaying how your teammate hogged the spotlight in a status meeting, it's probably affecting your work. If you're too distracted in a meeting to absorb key information or contribute to the discussion, your preoccupation with your colleague's behavior is diverting energy from your job.

How to decide

How can you be sure a difficult conversation is worth the risk? The problems we face at work come with a lot of gray area. You start with a point of contention and add to it layers of context and complexity such as hierarchy, roles, goals, frequency of interaction, and so on. Should you shirk sharing constructive feedback with a direct report even if they're moving on to a new role (and a new boss)? Probably not. Then, of course, there are those times when your counterpart takes the lead and launches a discussion. But for the occasions where you have the luxury of contemplating a difficult situation and weighing whether or not to address it, ask yourself:

- Does my short- or long-term success rely on ad- dressing this problem?

- Does the situation I'm facing concern a direct report or my boss?

- Is the relationship with this person short term (is it a one-time interaction or discrete project) or ongoing (for example, am I working with my boss's boss or a coworker I rely on to get my job done)?

- How important is it, to me and to the organization, to improve the relationship or the situation?

- Is the issue affecting my ability to concentrate or how I feel about going to work every day?

- Does the situation I'm grappling with involve other colleagues or customers?

Even if the answers to these questions reveal that the problem is a one-time occurrence or you don't interact frequently enough with the person in question to raise the issue now, things can change. Perhaps deciding not to address the issue will work, or it may only be effective for a short period of time, and then you'll find that you need to reassess the situation.

Don't put off a conversation just because it's hard

Sometimes your introspective review will yield conflicting results: Your brain is ready to address the issue, but your gut hesitates. It's natural to want to avoid difficult conversations even when we know we need to have them.

Say your project is coming in over budget. You may be inclined to delay telling your boss the bad news. You assume she'll be furious, and she'll find out soon enough anyway. But when you reflect on the fact that this is your boss and that you want her to trust you to handle crises well, you'll realize that even though it won't be easy to break the bad news, it's much better to let her know what's happening. After she blows off steam, you'll be able to talk about solutions and work together to limit the damage. (See table 2, "Bad reasons for avoiding a hard conversation—and some solutions.)"

TABLE 2

Bad reasons for avoiding a hard conversation—and some solutions

Reason	Action
You fear conflict.	Acknowledge that even though conflict can be uncomfortable, it's inevitable and a normal part of work life. Looking at what's going on beneath the surface can help you focus on the root cause and reduce your discomfort.
You deny there's a problem.	Think about your workplace relationships. Notice which ones seem tense, frustrating, or unproductive. Consider how those negative factors are holding you back from doing your best work and collaborating effectively.
You're sure the other person won't change.	Your goal isn't to change anyone or to assign blame. You want to improve your interactions. You can do that by adjusting your mind-set and modifying your behavior.
You think you can work around it.	Assess whether the benefits of an improved situation outweigh the risks of addressing the problem. If they do, prepare for a conversation. If they don't, keep tabs on how the relationship evolves; you may need to revisit your approach.
You think the problem will solve itself.	Most problems don't just go away. If ignored, they can get worse. Engaging in a skillful conversation can move you closer to a positive solution.

When you decide to have a difficult conversation

If, after honest reflection, you decide it's in your best interest to initiate a discussion, it's time to proactively work on building a productive mind-set by examining your emotions.

Name what you feel

In his groundbreaking research, psychologist Daniel Goleman identifies "emotional intelligence" as the key driver of success at work. Emotional intelligence is the ability to sense and respond to the interpersonal dimension of a relationship or situation. Developing an understanding of your inner landscape (and that of your colleagues) will help you build more positive professional interactions in general—and that includes being able to navigate difficult conversations.

According to Goleman, the first quality of emotional intelligence is self-awareness. How do you start to change the way you interact with a colleague in a difficult situation if you don't understand your own feelings and what's key to your self-image? Your self-image is a set of core traits that you believe characterize who you are. If you've never thought about those traits, you won't be prepared to respond if they're threatened. For example, if you believe that striving for excellence is core to your identity, you're probably sensitive when someone points out an error or oversight on your watch. "My boss returned the report I drafted all marked up! She thinks I'm incompetent!" You react strongly because fundamental emotional needs, such as being valued and respected, underlie your self-image.

Perhaps you and your teammate, Andrea, have been knocking heads about how and when to deliver project updates to a client. Is it possible that on top of the process disagreement, you feel threatened by

Andrea because she has an MBA and you don't? By naming what you feel, the emotion loosens its grip on you: "I feel jealous of Andrea because she has an MBA and often uses big words to argue for her point of view. I can't cite case studies or research, but I know that the deep understanding of customers I've gained from the hours I've spent answering the help desk phones is valuable. Still, I feel too insecure, and even ashamed, to assert my view."

Naming your feelings might not come naturally to you. Thinking back to what we discussed in the first chapter about different personal styles, it's clear that some people are more comfortable talking about their emotions than others. If you don't think or talk about your emotions much, stop and reflect on whether they're keeping you from addressing an issue in a productive way. Sometimes it helps to write them down or keep a journal, especially if you're anticipating a difficult conversation. You may think you're annoyed about your colleague's bombastic behavior, but on reflection, are you feeling something else, such as embarrassed or betrayed? Often an easily labeled emotion—angry, sad, disappointed—masks other, more complex ones. You thought you were mad that you weren't tapped to attend the trade fair, but are you really feeling inadequate?

By identifying the subtle feelings (or layers of feelings) that color all of your interactions, you'll be more aware of them when they arise and gain a little emotional distance from them. If you were recently promoted to team leader, for example, you probably feel pleased and proud. But you may also feel a bit uncomfortable around your former teammates, because your promotion changes the reporting relationships. Maybe you start avoiding them on breaks; you sense that they're dodging you, too. The promotion might have triggered insecurity. Are you really up to the new job? Do your former teammates see you as a fraud? Looking for patterns in your reactions to people and situations raises your awareness of your own particular vulnerabilities. Certain colleagues and scenarios may trigger tough emotions for you; they threaten your self-image. As you begin to understand your reactions and acknowledge that they stem from human needs, you'll start to develop skills and strategies to keep your emotions in balance when facing these triggering people or situations—making challenging conversations less difficult and more productive.

Once you've named what you're feeling in the situation at hand and explored the complicated emotions underlying your reaction, you'll be able to see whether—and how—your own feelings may have clouded your judgment about the issue. Resist judging yourself, and accept that you, like everyone, have blind spots. This will help you move beyond your knee-jerk reactions—I'm right, she's wrong—and be open to considering other factors.

Take the initiative

It takes two people to have a conversation, so it's counterintuitive to think that one person alone will change the outcome. But in fact that's absolutely true. No matter how toxic a relationship seems, through awareness and discipline, each person has the ability to change his or her own behavior. By changing your own mind-set, you greatly increase the odds of having a constructive conversation, even when you have to deliver bad news. Once you begin to examine your assumptions, emotions, and habitual thoughts, you'll quickly notice how your original view of the problem is transformed. You'll become an agent of change instead of a victim of circumstance.

So far all of your work has been introspective: understanding the root cause of the problem and the layers of emotion you're feeling. In the next chapter we'll look at how to widen your focus to include what's going on for your counterpart. You'll learn to plan a conversation that meets not only your needs but also those of the other person—and of the larger organization.

Prepare for
the Difficult
Conversation

Prepare for the Difficult Conversation

N ow that you've decided to initiate a difficult conversation and considered the emotional factors at play, what additional steps can you take to ensure a successful outcome? Of course you can't know what your counterpart will say. But taking some time on your own to think things through may mean the difference between losing your cool and maintaining your focus to reach a positive resolution. Whether a difficult conversation will be successful depends on how well you prepare before you walk into the room—specifically, your understanding of your own state of mind and your ability to think through how you'll frame the conversation. We'll follow the story of Liam and Shireen, account reps on the same regional team, to see what this looks like in practice.

Liam has been on the team for a few years; Shireen was recently hired. In her first team meeting, Shireen managed to turn a simple request to "tell us a bit about yourself" into a lengthy exposition of her professional accomplishments. Then a colleague overheard her taking personal credit for work the whole team had done. After a few months of working with Shireen, Liam's nerves are on edge. Even though the new hire isn't targeting Liam personally, he feels he needs to defend his own work and the team's by sending update e-mails to senior management documenting how everyone is contributing to the project's success. Liam knows he will have to continue to work with Shireen: Not only are they on the same team, they sit in an open workspace, and their market segments overlap. He suspects she's checking out his client list. He feels he needs to say something to her, but how should he do it? What should he say?

Assess the facts—and your assumptions

Before we engage in a two-way conversation, we only have access to our own thoughts and observations to interpret events. The first step in conducting a difficult conversation productively is to review all the pertinent information. What seems like a problem to you may be business as usual to your counterpart.

Ask yourself:

- Are there relevant factors you don't know about?

- Are past experiences coloring your interpretation of events?

- Are you making unwarranted negative assumptions about the other person's motives?

Shireen is driving Liam crazy, but why? Liam can use these reflective questions to help him take a closer look at his view of the situation. Is it that he's simply bothered by her grandstanding? Is it that she's exceeding her sales goals and making the rest of the team look bad? Or is there a real risk that Shireen will poach Liam's accounts? As he's doing this reality check to prepare for the discussion, Liam should share his views with a neutral party. It may be that Liam's impressions are distorted or that he's overreacting, and a neutral opinion makes that evident.

Liam should also consider what else is affecting Shireen's behavior. Did their manager set aggressive goals for her first three months? What first impressions did she have of the department? Perhaps she noticed how tight-knit the team was and figured she had to make a big impression. And what assumptions is she making about Liam? Did she identify him as the unspoken leader of the team, aloof and unapproachable? As Liam plays out possible scenarios in his mind, his view of the problem expands.

Once Liam has reviewed the possible facts and checked his assumptions, he should think about what he wants to achieve from the conversation. Changing Shireen's nature, which Liam perceives as flamboyant, isn't a realistic goal. But finding a way to ease the tension, get to know each other better, and collaborate more effectively is within reach.

Again, each of us only experiences a situation from our unique perspective. But when we acknowledge that for each person the view and the facts look different, a difficult conversation becomes an opportunity to express and reconcile both individuals' perceptions and forge a mutually acceptable way forward.

Address the emotions

To begin to manage the strong emotions you're likely to experience in a challenging interpersonal situation, start by acknowledging that the situation is charged, not only for you, but probably for your counterpart, too.

In Liam's case his preoccupation with Shireen's behavior is affecting his performance. He has fallen behind on client calls. He needs to get a handle on how his emotions are exacerbating the situation. Here are some things to consider.

Is my self-image threatened?

Earlier in the book we talked about understanding what's core to our sense of who we are. As you prepare a difficult conversation, one of the first things to look for is whether it feels like your self-image is under attack.

For Liam, it's possible that Shireen's behavior is simply an irritant, like a fly buzzing around, just out of reach. But maybe there's something deeper going on. On reflection, Liam sees that after having met his goals for months, Shireen was hired and within days began commanding the spotlight. That felt unfair! Liam knows that a key component of his self-image is competence. He wants to be valued for his reliable, consistent performance. When he hears Shireen touting her successes and soliciting praise for them, he feels inadequate and underappreciated.

What about my counterpart's emotions?

As hard as it may seem, when you're preparing for a difficult conversation it's essential to think about how the other person might be feeling. Could Shireen's bravado be a cover-up for some insecurity on her part? Is she feeling isolated, given that she's joining a well-established team and others aren't sharing critical client information? Now it occurs to Liam that she's been overtalking and looks uncomfortable after team meetings. Maybe she's not so sure of herself after all. Trying to view the situation from your counterpart's perspective will help you develop the empathy needed to have a successful conversation.

What feelings could the conversation trigger?

When emotions run high, we tend to think of any in-teraction as a battlefield where one side wins and the other side loses. Whatever the other person says feels like a personal attack. Not to respond in kind seems like surrendering.

This zero-sum thinking boxes us in and never leads to more than short-term gains. What if Shireen bursts out, "At my first team meeting I felt like I was walking the plank. No one smiled and you in particular glared at me the whole time." If Liam fires back, "That's bull! You're the one who swept in like it was a coronation! You alienated everybody in the first five minutes," the conversation has already gone off the rails. When pre-paring for the discussion, Liam would do better to dispel the notion that any valid point Shireen makes is a loss for him. If he is able to avoid taking the bait if she says something inflammatory and defuse his own feelings of insecurity, he will create space for a more productive way forward.

Acknowledge that you're part of the problem

When you look honestly at how your thoughts and emotions are contributing to a potentially volatile situation, you will enter into a related discussion with greater calm and moderation. Liam should think about how and why he didn't share key company information with Shireen during her first days on the job. At what point did he decide she was an adversary? When had he begun avoiding her and cutting her off when she tried to speak in status meetings? Maybe Shireen's self-confidence and enthusiasm are a tough fit with Liam's own low-key, slightly sardonic style. Liam might have quickly but unconsciously decided to teach Shireen a lesson in humility by avoiding and interrupting her. Becoming aware of the way his own behavior has contributed to the current situation may change the picture for Liam and help him see Shireen as a person with legitimate needs, feelings, and insecurities rather than as the enemy.

As you prepare for your conversation, it's helpful to make a simple diagram of the basic issues and emotions as you identify them and as you imagine your counterpart sees them. An example of Liam's diagram is shown in table 3, "Perceived issues and emotions."

TABLE 3

Perceived issues and emotions

	Liam's view	Liam's perception of Shireen's view
The problem	Shireen isn't a team player. She's making me look bad.	I need to make a strong impression to establish myself.
The feelings	Underneath my anger I feel jealous of her success and threatened by it.	I feel isolated and insecure because my coworkers are unwelcoming.

Identify a range of positive outcomes

By examining your perspective and that of your counterpart, you're already looking at a richer context—one that allows for a wider range of contributing factors and possible results. Now ask yourself what you hope to achieve by initiating the conversation. Be specific. You may want to improve the relationship in a long-range sense, but be clear about the objectives of this particular conversation. The more focused your goals, the more likely you are to achieve them. Identify your preferred outcome, but consider other results that would work for you as well.

Do a reality check of your goals against the other person's perspective. In Liam's case he wants Shireen to agree to share the spotlight and the credit. But when Liam considers Shireen's needs and perspective, he's able to move beyond what he wants personally and generate possibilities that might be acceptable to both of them.

Charting potential positive outcomes of a conversation, as shown in table 4, "Two views, multiple outcomes," will help you articulate your perspective and envision your counterpart's point of view.

TABLE 4

Two views, multiple outcomes

	Liam's view	Liam's perception of Shireen's view
Best outcome	Shireen acknowledges that she isn't sharing the spotlight. She agrees to work to share more credit with me and the team.	Liam acknowledges that my work is valuable and that I have a contribution to make. He agrees to support my success.
Possible alternate outcome	Shireen is willing to share account information with me before the next department meeting.	I'll set up informal one-on-one meetings with team members to improve my relationships with them.
Possible alternate outcome	Shireen agrees that we got off to a rocky start. We schedule a follow-up conversation.	Liam shared some legitimate concerns. I'd like to talk with him again soon to make sure he knows where I'm coming from.

Develop a strategy, not a script

Once you uncover the basic issues and emotions involved for both parties and consider what you want to achieve, you're ready to envision how the conversation might unfold. Plan for different scenarios based on several ways your counterpart could respond. If you're nervous, do a dry run in front of a mirror, practicing neutral facial expressions and open body language. Try a mock conversation with a family member or other unbiased party in which you imagine and verbalize both sides of a hypothetical discussion. This will help you as you gather and focus your thoughts before you sit down. (See the sidebar "Questions to help you prepare for the conversation.")

While it's critical to prepare, it's not in your best interest to develop a script. As soon as your counterpart says something "off script," you might lose your balance. Instead, envision the conversation as a meeting

QUESTIONS TO HELP YOU PREPARE
FOR THE CONVERSATION

- What is the issue I'm trying to resolve?

- What is my counterpart's view of the issue?

- What assumptions are we making about the situation and each other?

- What underlying interests are at stake for me? For my counterpart?

- What feelings does the situation trigger for me? For my counterpart?

- What do I want to achieve from the conversation?

- How can we break the impasse?

place where both people have the freedom to express their positions and their needs, listen to each other, and feel respected.

The goal is not to "win a round" but to move the conversation and the relationship forward. Liam should consider how best to frame the issue and how to respond to Shireen's possible responses. He can decide what points he wants to make and what questions to ask and come up with some mutually beneficial solutions to propose. He'll be approaching the issue with a new mind-set and allowing for a range of positive next steps.

To start the conversation, it's probably not a good idea for Liam to blurt out, "Hey, new girl, didn't you ever learn the rules of schoolyard etiquette?" Instead, he'll lead with something neutral, such as, "Shireen, I think you and I may have gotten off on the wrong foot. I'd like to talk about how we can work together better and make the team more successful." In that case she's more likely to respond along the lines of, "Liam, I'm glad you brought it up. I've been feeling some tension, too. Let's talk about it."

Consider the timing of the conversation. If your emotions are running high for any reason, it's best to wait. Acknowledging that your feelings play a key role isn't the same as letting them rule. Likewise, select a neutral setting for the conversation where neither person will feel exposed or have an unfair advantage.

Following these steps sets the stage for a discussion in which both people feel respected and genuinely heard and that a better way forward is possible. Now that you've carefully prepared the conversation you want to have, it's time to put your new skills and understanding into practice. In the following chapter, we'll see how.

Conduct the Conversation

Conduct the Conversation

You've planned a conversation where both you and the other person are able to express yourselves and contribute to a solution. Now, how do you start the conversation, and how do you keep it on track?

Here's where the external work begins—the part where you leave the relative comfort of your own thoughts and actually invite the other person to join the conversation. But the thorough internal work you've done will help you keep your focus on the positive outcomes you now know are possible.

A difficult conversation might unfold like this. You and Kate are part of a cross-functional team. You're responsible for the design of a new software product. Kate is managing the publicity rollout. For the past month, Kate has pressed you at weekly status meetings to agree to hard-and-fast milestones for the social media campaign. "The client needs interim dates to nail down his ad buys. We can't keep putting him off!" You've already explained that every step is predicated on successfully testing the previous stage. "I'll commit to holding the release date," you say, "but until then we have to be able to respond to surprises." The tension between you and Kate has been building. At last week's meeting she burst out, "You're sabotaging the marketing launch! Commit to some dates already!"

You've decided to address the problem in a one-on-one conversation with Kate. You've carefully thought through the issues, Kate's possible perspectives and interests, and what you hope to gain from the conversation. You've invited her to meet at a quiet coffee station in another part of the building. How do you begin the conversation?

Acknowledge the other person

No matter how prepared you are, it's hard to find the words to start the conversation with the right tone. You're prepared to talk about the issue, but you can't be sure that your counterpart is.

It's never wrong to start with a simple thank you. Thanking the other person for agreeing to speak with you will signal that you respect her time and her agreement to engage. It's helpful to make eye contact and start with a smile—even though that won't come naturally in every situation. A smile signals your willingness to be open.

Start by acknowledging your counterpart and letting her know that you see her as a person with legitimate needs and motivations. If you don't signal your respect and instead dive right into the substance of your issue, the conversation might quickly go in an unintended direction.

You: I've been meaning to talk with you for weeks. Your insistence on interim dates is frankly unacceptable. You must realize how impossible that is for design.

Kate: *My* demands are unacceptable? Whose head will roll when the marketing launch tanks? You're not giving me anything to work with!

Oops—that approach really bombed. Kate felt attacked and immediately went on the offensive. Your opening words set up a classic I'm-right-you're-wrong conversation in which both sides will dig in their heels and wage a war of attrition.

Now consider an alternate scenario:

You: Kate, I want to thank you for agreeing to talk with me today. I realize it's an especially busy time, and you probably have plenty of things on your plate.

Kate: It's true that I'm counting down to this huge launch—my inbox is overflowing. But it seems like you have something important on your mind.

This time the conversation is off to a better start. Your simple acknowledgment of Kate's time and effort set the stage for a respectful exchange.

Frame the problem

You've acknowledged that your counterpart's time is valuable. Now reinforce your respectful approach by quickly describing the issue from your perspective. Observe her body language as you speak. If she looks surprised or put off by something you say, pause to explicitly check your assumptions. Ask if you missed or misinterpreted something. Keep your tone neutral and your body language open: Your aim is to foster a constructive dialogue, not score points. Here are a few guidelines for describing your version of the problem.

Use "I"

It's good practice to explicitly describe your views using "I" statements. This shows that you're not assuming your perspective is the truth of the situation. It also demonstrates that you're acknowledging your role in the problem and not assigning blame.

Here's a way to use "I" statements to frame the problem for Kate:

> *You:* I'd like to talk with you about something that's been weighing on me. It's about the tension that's been building between the design team's needs for flexibility and the marketing team's requests for interim dates.

> *Kate:* You're right that there's tension there. I'm feeling it, too.

Express your feelings

Describing how you view the problem naturally allows you to articulate what you're feeling. It reminds your counterpart that you're experiencing strong emotions, too. It also gives you an opening to acknowledge that your emotional reactions are part of the problem. You've examined your emotions to prepare for this conversation. Now the key is to talk about your feelings without being overwhelmed by them.

> *You:* I'm worried about this situation. I see that the tension between our departments is affecting my morale and the team's. I want to be a team player, and I'm committed to delivering a great product. I know I've been hesitant to agree in the status meetings to interim dates. But if I make promises I can't keep, I'll be letting everyone down, and it will reflect badly on Design and on the project. I feel my credibility is on the line.

> *Kate:* I hadn't thought of that. I've been so anxious about the marketing launch and all the client and partner demands that I've had a bit of a one-track mind. My reputation is on the line, too.

Focus on issues, not personalities

The fastest way to trigger a defensive response from the other person is to cast her as the source of the problem. To stay balanced and avoid flared tempers, talk about the issues without attributing them to your counterpart's behavior or her personality. In the conversation with Kate, you've successfully avoided calling out what you view as her blunt style and overbearing attitude. Instead, you've focused on the competing priorities between Marketing and Design rather than the tension between the two of you.

Ask questions and listen

You've set a positive tone for the conversation, framed your view of the issues, and described your feelings. Now you need to invite the other person to do the same. By explicitly asking for her version of the situation, you reinforce the message that the conversation is an opportunity to jointly problem solve, not just a chance to vent.

Let's turn to another hypothetical example to illustrate the critical role of asking questions and listening carefully in a difficult conversation.

Vivek is an HR recruiter for a large health insurance provider. He's trying to fill a support position for Nina, a demanding new-accounts manager. The market for recent graduates is tight, and this job description is pretty generic. Nina has already rejected a dozen résumés that Vivek prescreened. This morning he found a curt message in his inbox: "New clients are waiting for their policies to take effect while you fill my inbox with subpar candidates. When are you planning to step up your game?"

Vivek takes a breath. He's been the target of Nina's sarcasm in the past, and he's always succeeded in ignoring it. But this is beyond the pale. How can he continue to work with a person who is so blatantly contemptuous? Vivek doesn't report to Nina, but Nina is a rising star in her division, and he fills positions for her regularly. Vivek resolves to talk with her.

Nina, for her part, keeps coworkers at arm's length, and is quite happy when they return the favor. She has no use for small talk, especially with someone like Vivek, whom she thinks of as a timid drone. When Vivek asks her for a brief meeting, Nina balks at what she views as more wasted time. She accepts the invitation begrudgingly.

When they sit down to talk, it's clear that Vivek is well prepared. He starts by thanking Nina for her time, and she's impressed by his confident manner. Even so, Nina bristles as Vivek starts to describe his perspective: "I want to talk about the problems I'm having filling your open position," he explains, "and the tension I feel building up around it." *What business does this underling have complaining when I'm the one with a whole department to worry about?* thinks Nina. But when Vivek says he's currently working on nine open positions, he's got her attention. She's never considered that Vivek has competing priorities, too. Then, as he shows her statistics indicating that the job market for entry-level positions is the tightest it's been in five years, she begins to soften.

Now Vivek says, "Nina, I've told you what's going on for me and why I felt upset and resentful when I read your e-mail. Can you help me better understand how you view the situation?"

By the time Nina hears this question, she's already seeing a bigger picture and for the first time thinking of Vivek as a competent professional with competing priorities of his own. Now she's relieved to have a chance to share how much pressure she's under. Nina explains, "Well, I've been feeling overwhelmed by the workload and there's no one to delegate to. My boss doesn't cut me any slack. I need to get this position filled so that our department keeps functioning." Nina feels validated as she sees Vivek listening and nodding.

So far, Vivek has done a good job of setting up a positive conversation. He was well prepared and presented the issue calmly, sticking to the issues and scrupulously avoiding any assignment of blame. By asking Nina to share her version of events, Vivek invites her to be a partner in the conversation, not an adversary. Once Nina gives her side of the story, Vivek can restate his understanding of the situation and ask questions to fill in any blanks. He'll be able to express empathy by letting Nina know he understands how much pressure she's under. By mirroring back his understanding of Nina's version of the story, Vivek lends it legitimacy. Nina starts to feel like she, too, has something to gain from the conversation.

Listening carefully and showing your counterpart that you're genuinely trying to understand her position will give you information you were missing before. And it may well defuse her emotions enough to let her consider a new way forward. When that happens, you're ready to start exploring solutions together.

Look for common ground

We know that the source of a problem is often competing interests or different views of the relevant facts. If you point out where you and your counterpart's interests align, you'll open a fruitful avenue for discussion.

Vivek and Nina have at least one common interest: They both want to get Nina's position filled quickly. To acknowledge that, Vivek says, without sarcasm, "Believe me, the faster I fill your position the happier I'll be. Then I'll only need to worry about the other eight!" This lightens the moment and starts building small bridges between the two positions.

Vivek points out other common interests, too, such as meeting quarterly goals: "My target is to have a number of positions filled, while yours is to have a number of new accounts set up. Filling this position advances both of our objectives." Vivek then invites Nina to share her ideas about the best way to collaborate to fill the position. Nina provides a more detailed candidate profile and emphasizes stretch goals in the job description. She explores the possibility of expanding the salary range and including an explicit professional development component. Vivek will be more likely to attract ambitious and well-qualified candidates by pointing out these opportunities.

Adapt and rebalance

Despite your best intentions and careful preparation, real-life conversations rarely go according to plan. At any point along the way you may be surprised by something your counterpart says or how he says it. You may also find that your own emotions flare up, causing confusion or a strong internal reaction of anger or embarrassment that pushes you to want to lash out or stomp off. But you can regain your composure and get back on track by anticipating some possible reactions. Here are tips for managing common scenarios that could throw you off:

- *You get angry.* No matter how diplomatic you try to be, your counterpart may respond harshly to something you say. If the other person says, "I didn't expect much better from you," you'll probably feel your anger flare. At moments like this, don't take the bait, take a breath. If you still want to fight back, take another breath. You may feel the anger subside. Chances are you'll remember your intentions and return to managing the conversation in a positive way. If you need more time to balance your emotions, ask to reschedule: "Wow! I'm feeling very reactive right now, and I think whatever I say or do won't move the conversation forward. How about getting together tomorrow morning at the same time?"

- *She gets angry.* You can't control the other person's reactions, but you can control yours. Stay calm, and maintain a neutral tone. "It seems like this is bringing up some strong feelings for you. Can you help me understand why?" If your counterpart can begin to explain, she'll probably cool down in the process. If not, ask whether she wants to table the conversation for now and meet at another time. Let her be the one to decide.

- *You feel misunderstood.* Something the person said shows that he's not hearing you. He seems stuck on one passing remark you made, and he's not addressing what you see as the root issue. He may feel threatened by you, and his emotions are preventing him from really listening. Maybe he doesn't trust that you're being sincere or telling the whole story. Or perhaps he hasn't let go of his preconceived ideas about you or the problem. Acknowledge that you're concerned that you haven't been clear. Ask what else he wants to know. The more input you elicit, and the more you show you're really trying to understand, the more likely it is that he'll get beyond his preconceptions and really listen to you. "I sense that I'm not making myself clear enough. How can I give you the information you need?"

- *You don't know where she stands.* Despite your careful planning and the good work you've done framing the issue, let's say you find yourself baffled by your counterpart's response. Maybe she's very quiet, and you can't pick up any cues. Or she's very conciliatory, but you sense it's not authentic. Ask more questions, and check your understanding. "I'm trying to understand your perspective on this, but I'm not quite there yet. Did you say you felt I was stalling when I asked for more details about the job description? Can you say why?" Keeping the dialog open is the only way to reach a breakthrough.

- *He digs in his heels.* If you're trying to generate solutions but you sense that your counterpart still feels his way is the only way, acknowledge that his position and concerns are legitimate. Ask how he thinks things could be better. Then return the discussion to common interests. Even focusing on one common goal gives the other person an opening to acknowledge that creative solutions are possible. Perhaps you're conducting market research on a new product and the product manager is insisting that focus groups are a waste of time and money: "You mentioned earlier that the last two focus groups didn't give us useful data. Could we provide more context by adding a control group?" You could also try to break the impasse by offering something. "You said the schedule is under pressure because we need a third round of testing. We could save a couple of weeks by running the last two focus groups concurrently."

Unexpected things can and will happen during a conversation. But when they do, <u>don't panic.</u> Every difficult moment is a chance to practice your skills. Use the presence of mind and flexibility you've learned to stay neutral and pivot to higher ground.

Establish commitments

As the conversation continues, you will have already begun to touch on possible ways forward. Now it's time to see which ones to flesh out and agree on. Solutions will vary widely according to the specifics of your situation. Some issues are so complicated or so entrenched that the most you should hope to achieve in the first conversation is a commitment to talk again. "I feel good about our conversation. I'd like to mull over what I've learned and talk again in a few days. Would you be open to that?"

Sometimes you can do more: "We agreed to share biweekly updates to ensure we're showing the client a unified front." If you can end the conversation with at least one shared commitment and agreed-upon next step and state them clearly to ensure your counterpart signs on, you'll have made real progress. You managed the conversation successfully. Now you need to secure that progress by following through on what you've agreed.

Follow Through

Follow Through

You made it through the conversation—congratulations! The time and effort you invested in thinking through and preparing for the interaction paid off. You avoided land mines, maintained a constructive tone, and agreed on at least one next step. Hopefully your counterpart shares your positive assessment. But there's still work to do. It's very possible that the conversation ended before you could flesh out the details of an action plan. Or maybe you came away thinking that there were important points you didn't bring up or you wish you had been able to respond to the other person more effectively. Now comes the essential work of solidifying and building on the gains you made in the conversation to ensure a more productive working relationship going forward.

How did you do?

When you debrief after the conversation, ask yourself tough questions about how well you met the goals you initially set. How do you feel? Are you relieved? Are you optimistic about the prospect of future collaboration with this person? Do you think he feels the same way? Or do you feel bruised and disappointed? In either case, it's critical to explore why you feel the way you do. Otherwise you've missed an opportunity to gather important information for the next difficult conversation. Here are some useful questions to ask as you assess the effectiveness of the discussion:

- Do I feel proud of how I managed the conversation? Do I feel strong? Or do I feel let down, embattled, embarrassed—or just happy it's over?

- Did I meet the objectives and cover the topics I outlined for myself?

- Did I present my perspective in ways that are consistent with my intentions?

- Did I show respect?

- Do I feel differently now about the person or the problem?

- Did I learn anything that changes my view of the problem?

Let's say you asked your boss for a raise. Despite your thorough preparation, the conversation was tough, you never got your groove, and it didn't end with a clear answer. If, even with an inconclusive result, you came away from the conversation feeling pretty good about the way you handled it, you have a solid base to build on whatever comes next. If you don't feel so good about it, you have plenty of grist for learning. Identify the source of your disappointment. Then go back and think through what you'll do differently the next time.

Jot down your impressions

As quickly as possible, carve out time to make detailed but informal notes about the conversation. It's important to do this soon after the conversation, before your memory fades and interpretations set in. Try to remember as many specifics as you can. Write down your impressions, starting with what gestures or exchanges you remember most vividly. For example, you could write:

My hands were sweating, and I felt my forehead burning. At first I talked too fast, and she avoided eye contact. Then she made a joke and that broke the ice. I remembered the arguments I'd planned to use to support my request for a raise and started to feel more confident. But she didn't smile much, and I felt unsure of myself right to the end.

Another, more thorough method is to group your notes by category. (See table 5, "Notes about the conversation," for a sample grid of how to document the conversation with your boss about a raise.)

Pushing yourself to write down as much detail as possible about your side of the conversation—and what you perceived from the other person—will help you remember and then take into account information that you might not otherwise have captured. Doing so will keep you moving toward solutions to the issue you're facing and avoid going over the same ground during future encounters. Writing down your impressions will also help you meet your long-term goal to become a better communicator so that difficult conversations become less frequent and easier to manage. We'll focus more on that in the next chapter.

TABLE 5

Notes about the conversation

	Mine	Hers
Body language	Felt hot, sat stiffly. Used my hands a lot. Slowly became calmer. Tried to smile, but it wasn't spontaneous.	Closed at first, then more relaxed and open. Occasional smile.
Tone of voice	High and rushed at first. Gradually took on a more normal tone but still talked too fast.	Cool, didn't vary much.
Emotions	Nervous, self-conscious, embarrassed. Had trouble reading her reaction, which made me feel insecure.	Seemed calm, objective, a little impatient toward the end.
Description of problem	Probably didn't have enough specific arguments. Focused too much on tenure, not enough on merit?	Talked about changes in the department and new company goals. Didn't respond directly to my points.
Objectives stated	Led with the request for a raise. Tried to keep the focus on that, but maybe lost the thread?	Didn't respond with a yes or no answer, but said she was looking at the overall department.
Questions asked or missed	Didn't ask about what department changes she's considering and why.	Asked why I thought I should get a raise, but didn't ask follow-up questions.

Listening	So nervous and flustered that I had a hard time focusing on what she said.	Kept eye contact and seemed to listen.
Common ground	Had a one-track mind. Hard to concentrate on other issues she brought up.	Said a decision about my raise would be in the context of overall changes in the department.
Solutions proposed	Requested that we meet again when she has more information.	Said she'd have more information in the next few weeks.

Follow up in writing

You've debriefed and documented the conversation for yourself. Now reach out to your counterpart in writing. Start by thanking her for the time and effort it took to meet. Then reiterate at least one point she made to demonstrate that you heard her, and succinctly summarize the next steps as you understand them.

This last part is crucial. It's possible that even though you thought you'd agreed on an action plan, her view differs. In the case of the inconclusive conversation with your boss about a raise, you left with the impression that she was considering your request. But she may assume that you understood that the answer was no, or at least not now. By writing a follow-up e-mail and explicitly stating your takeaway, you increase the likelihood that she'll either confirm your assumption or elaborate further.

Draft a brief e-mail, summarizing your assessment of the agreement. Ask for a date or a timeline within which she'll give you an answer. For example: "Janice, thanks for taking the time to meet with me yesterday to discuss my request for a raise. I understand that you're looking at roles and responsibilities in light of company goals for the coming fiscal year. You said you'd know more in the coming weeks. Could you get back to me by the first of next month?" Or ask for a follow-up conversation to establish what you'll need to do to be considered for the raise or a promotion.

If in reviewing the conversation you felt that you neglected to mention key points or somehow got off track, now is your opportunity to keep the discussion going. In this case write a quick note or e-mail to invite your counterpart to meet again. For instance: "Janice, thanks for meeting with me yesterday to discuss my request for a raise. In reviewing my notes I realized there were a few items I neglected to address that I'd like you to consider. Can we have a quick follow-up meeting at your convenience?" Don't be afraid to admit that you forgot a few points you wanted to make or that you were flustered. The key is to show that you're motivated to share all the relevant information and maintain a positive dialog.

Keep your commitments

In the best case, you've ended the conversation with one or more clear action steps. Just as you expect your counterpart to make good on her promises, you need to thoroughly fulfill and even exceed yours. If your boss agrees to meet in a month and asks you to produce a memo summarizing your accomplishments and making your case for the raise, have it on her desk on Monday morning. Document your stretch goals. Brainstorm a list of ways to increase your responsibilities and be more valuable to the department and to your boss. Your actions communicate even more than your words. This is your opportunity to demonstrate your merit, bolster your request, and pave the way for the next conversation.

Likewise, if you conducted a tough performance review with a direct report, it's incumbent on you to be explicit about how he needs to improve and when and how you'll assess his progress. You may feel relieved that the conversation went reasonably well and that he took the feedback constructively. But how you follow up is as important as the conversation itself. If the employee asked for a weekly one-on-one meeting to assess his progress leading up to the next formal review, carve out the time for those meetings and commit to making them productive. Be specific: "Alex, I'm looking forward to our check-ins. How about a brief meeting in my office every Monday at eleven?" If you asked him to provide regular status reports, read them and provide timely feedback: "Thanks for letting me know about the spreadsheet you created to track new leads. I'm looking forward to reviewing with you whether it generates new clients." Set a date for the next formal performance review so he knows what timeframe he's working with. Agree on how you'll measure success, and communicate about expectations.

Whatever the specific content of your conversation, following up on the commitments you made and being explicit in your expectations for next steps completes your work on the original conversation and sets the stage for productive future interactions.

Become a Better Communicator

Become a Better Communicator

You've accomplished a lot. You took the initiative to have a difficult conversation, did the work to make it as successful as possible, and followed up in ways that advance the issue and strengthen the relationship. You can do more. Continue to develop your new skills and prepare for your next challenging interaction. Communicating successfully means consistently deploying the self-knowledge and interpersonal skills we've been discussing throughout this book. Here are a few key habits to develop.

Reflect before you speak

Earlier in the book we discussed how changing a difficult dynamic requires emotional intelligence. At the core of that intelligence is self-awareness. Make a habit of asking yourself what kind of person you want to be and how you want others to perceive you. Then identify any gaps between how you want others to perceive you and what you actually say and do.

Of course, you're a complex person whose motivations, perceptions, and behaviors vary over time and according to the situation. People rarely perceive you as you see yourself, despite your best intentions. You have your internal filters and roadblocks, and your coworkers have theirs. To cut through the layers of interpretation, communicate as authentically as possible—and back up your words with actions that reinforce them. To develop this consistency, regularly ask yourself these simple questions:

- Who do I want to be?

- How do I want to behave in this situation?

- What do I want others to take away about me?

By habitually pausing to reflect on how you want to behave in tough situations, you'll learn what your core values are, and your actions will more likely reflect them. Keep a daily or weekly journal of the interactions you find challenging. Before long you'll see patterns in your behavior and things you want to work on. Say you notice from reviewing your journal that you often feel impatient and respond irritably to your teammates during the 4 p.m. status meeting. Try taking a quick walk or eating a piece of fruit before the meeting and see if your mood and responses improve. As you pay attention to how you engage with others and how they respond, you'll begin to express yourself with a fundamental consistency that others will notice and respect. It's not about being smooth or talking a good game—it's about making it a priority to be your best self even in the most challenging situations.

Connect with others

Your professional success depends on your ability to collaborate with others: your boss and your immediate teammates, of course, but also the person in HR who fills your open positions, the account manager who provides your weekly numbers, the technician who supports your videoconferences, and the administrative assistant who schedules team meetings. Make it a priority to connect with your colleagues on a personal level. If you don't show interest in a person until you need his help or buy-in, he'll interpret your overture as self-interested. Take the time to get to know people before you need them, find opportunities to regularly express appreciation for others' work, and look for areas of common interest: maybe you're both into gardening, running, or soccer or both have toddlers. You'll demonstrate your respect for others and build a reservoir of goodwill to tap into when problems or situations of competing interests arise.

An important part of building trust is being consistent. Everyone has bad days or moments when we're singularly focused and come across as dismissive or rude. We all deal with occasional extenuating circumstances at home that affect our ability to be our best selves at work. But nothing damages trust like repeated passive-aggressive behavior or volatile moods. Own your occasional outbursts or snarky comments, and talk and joke about them. Then those behaviors won't define you in your coworkers' minds. When you make a habit of talking about what went wrong— "I lost it and yelled at you for double-booking that interview! Sorry!"—and your peers see that you recognize your own weaknesses and aren't afraid to be self-critical, they'll trust you to be fair and open when their interests conflict with yours.

Before you talk, listen

You'll learn more and gain insight more quickly by keeping quiet. Don't focus obsessively on what you want to say, as most of us usually do. Instead, develop a habit of slowing down, listening carefully to what's being said, and observing people's body language as they speak. You'll be better able to make essential connections and move to a place of deeper understanding.

As your coworkers begin to notice that you listen thoroughly before jumping into a conversation, they'll come to respect your assessment more and listen more closely to what you say. In this way, listening is more persuasive than speaking. Maybe that's not so surprising when we consider how important it is for each of us to feel validated. When your coworker observes you actively listening and genuinely trying to understand his words and his intentions, he'll be more likely to give you the benefit of the doubt in moments when things heat up.

Make your words count

It's easy to assume that others understand why you're saying or doing something, but we all know that no one's a mind reader. Maybe you realize on Sunday night that the yearly board meeting is on Friday, and the annual report must be on every board member's desk at least one day before that to give everyone time to review it. So you show up on a Monday morning and announce to your team, "I need to pull everyone off what they're doing to get the annual report to the printer." It's obvious to you that no other task is more of a priority than this one. But to your team members your announcement comes out of nowhere. They're busy working on their own projects and priorities, and they've planned out their week. Others are counting on them, too. Even though it will take time and may feel like an extra step, you owe it to your team to clearly state your goals and intentions. Making a habit of communicating openly will gain you the buy-in of your coworkers and help avoid misunderstandings.

A little humility helps, too. For example: "Good morning, everyone. I know I lose points for waiting until Monday morning to drop this bombshell, but we all need to clear the decks to get this annual report to the printer by Wednesday." Ask your team members what's on their desks, and brainstorm possible ways to satisfy all of the priorities without compromising the annual report. Think about enlisting some contract help for a few days or negotiate an extension on another project. Get support for your objectives by first acknowledging it's a big ask, and then jump in to help the team meet the new requirement.

It's also important to be succinct. Research shows that after listening to you for forty seconds, people tune out. This is where preparation makes the difference. You may think you do fine when you shoot from the hip, but in fact you're more likely to ramble or be thrown off by others' negative body language and nervously talk more to compensate. When you have an important point to communicate, whatever the venue, plan what you want to say, and keep it brief.

Establish a feedback loop

You move fast. You form impressions quickly and take mental shortcuts to keep from getting stuck in the weeds. Sometimes you communicate in shorthand or change course and forget to send an e-mail. You make a key decision with one or two colleagues on the way to a meeting, leaving others in the dark. If this way of working sounds familiar, it's time to take a closer look at how your behavior affects others. Is your "efficient" style leading to communication breakdowns?

If you want to make sure that you're coming across to others as you intend to and picking up cues from the people around you, make a habit of asking others for feedback. Identify a few individuals—your boss, a close colleague, someone from HR—to regularly reach out to after presentations or meetings. "What was your take on the body language during our status meeting this morning? Does Design have a problem with the new specifications?" If you're working on a specific project, it's good to ask a few key coworkers for one-time feedback. "We covered a lot of ground in a half hour. Did I communicate everything you needed from me during that videoconference?"

Habitually asking for feedback makes it known that doing so is acceptable and ensures that you learn about missteps or communication gaps while there's time to rectify them. Use frequent, informal quick feedback points after a conversation, meeting, or presentation, such as "What did I do well? What could I do better next time?" By asking these simple questions and accepting responses with interest and equanimity, you signal to others that you welcome feedback, both positive and negative, and that you genuinely want to communicate as thoroughly and effectively as you can.

Address problems head-on

Differences are more than okay; they are often catalysts for creativity and even breakthroughs. As you develop the habits we've discussed in this chapter—of checking your responses, making connections, listening respectfully, communicating concisely, and asking for feedback—you'll reduce the likelihood of difficult interactions arising. But when problems do come up, resist the temptation to avoid them or temporarily smooth things over. Instead, use the skills you've learned in this book to thoughtfully address the problem head-on.

By separating issues from personalities, managing complicated emotions, and framing problems as surmountable obstacles to the team's—or the organization's—success, you'll defuse tense situations and progressively become more comfortable with difficult interactions in general. As you begin to hear others' grievances or demands without taking them personally, you'll approach each challenging interaction as an opportunity for learning. And each time you successfully navigate a difficult conversation with respect and empathy, you'll feel—and *be*—more capable of competently taking on even the thorniest interactions when they arise.

Learn More

Quick hits

David, Susan. "Manage a Difficult Conversation with Emotional Intelligence." HBR.org, June 19, 2014.

Conflict can't be resolved with logic alone: You need to tend to the swirl of strong emotions, too. This practical article by coaching expert David shows you how to approach a conflict with greater emotional intelligence. You'll learn to recognize the emotions at play in your situation, understand why those emotions exist, assess the impact of those emotions, and develop strategies to manage them.

Goulston, Mark. "How Well Do You Communicate During Conflict?" HBR.org Assessment

This brief questionnaire by business psychiatrist Goulston will help you assess your communication skills during a conflict. Tailored results offer advice and additional resources for improvement. You'll get tips on being direct, sensitive, patient, open-minded, and sincere—all critical qualities for resolving misunderstandings and repairing relationships.

Hedges, Kristi. "Five Essential Communication Skills to Catapult Your Career." HBR.org Webinar, September 5, 2014.

Develop your ability to express yourself in a variety of scenarios with this webinar video and slideshow by communications expert Hedges. Learn five essential communication skills: creating an intentional presence, getting buy-in, presenting ideas confidently and succinctly to a senior audience, developing a virtual leadership style to connect over technology, and giving and receiving direct feedback. Complete with questions to ask yourself, real-life stories, and actionable advice, you'll learn strategies for making every conversation more productive.

Books

Halvorson, Heidi Grant. *No One Understands You and What to Do about It*. Boston: Harvard Business Review Press, 2015.

Halvorson introduces you to the various lenses that color your everyday interactions and explains how understanding those lenses will help you communicate more clearly. Her work is based on decades of research in psychology and social science. Using the advice Halvorson gives in this book, you'll be able to send the messages you intend to send and improve your personal relationships and authenticity.

Harvard Business Review Press. *HBR's 10 Must Reads on Emotional Intelligence*. Boston: Harvard Business Press, 2015.

Strengthening your emotional intelligence will help you in all areas of your work life, but it's especially useful when you must conduct a difficult conversation. Take a deep dive into this essential leadership competency with this compilation of HBR's best articles on the topic from experts in the field. It will inspire you to monitor and channel your moods and emotions, make smart, empathetic people decisions, manage conflict, and regulate emotions within your team.

Weeks, Holly. *Failure to Communicate: How Conversations Go Wrong and What You Can Do to Right Them.* Boston: Harvard Business Review Press, 2010.

Looking to overcome the combat mentality, emotional maelstrom, and confusion that can poison difficult conversations? Communications expert Weeks explains why we often rely on ineffective tactics when we're faced with difficult situations. You'll learn strategies for mitigating aggression and defensiveness, tips for avoiding the worst pitfalls, and come away with the skills you need to get through hard conversations with your reputation *and* relationships intact.

Classics

David, Susan and Christina Congleton. "Emotional Agility." *Harvard Business Review*, November 2013 (product #R1311L).

We know that the ability to manage one's thoughts and feelings—emotional agility—is essential to business success, but how do we actually develop it? Executive coaches David and Congleton offer practical methods for mindfully and productively approaching your inner emotions. You'll learn to recognize your patterns, label your thoughts and emotions, accept those feelings and thoughts, and act on your values. By gaining an understanding of how to anticipate and solve problems, you'll develop the emotional agility you need to successfully take on difficult conversations.

DeSteno, David. "Who Can You Trust?" *Harvard Business Review*, March 2014 (product #R1403K).

It's easier to resolve a problem through a difficult conversation at work if you have a high degree of trust with your counterpart. This article draws on emerging research to show how trustworthiness works and offers four points to keep in mind the next time you're deciding whether or not to trust a new partner: Integrity can vary, power *does* corrupt, confidence often masks incompetence, and it's OK to trust your gut. From the useful sidebar "How to Prompt Trustworthiness in Others," you'll also learn techniques to improve and foster others' trust in you. You'll benefit not only from conversations that are less stressful but also from enriched relationships in all areas of your work life.

Manzoni, Jean-François. "A Better Way to Deliver Bad News." Harvard Business Review, September 2002 (product #R0209J).

Giving difficult feedback is one of the most difficult conversations any manager faces. INSEAD professor Manzoni will help you change your mind-set in how you develop and deliver difficult feedback. You'll learn to recognize biases and reframe criticism in a way that opens up honest dialogue.

Sources

Primary source for this book

Harvard Business School Publishing. *Pocket Mentor: Managing Difficult Interactions*. Boston: Harvard Business School Press, 2008.

Other sources consulted

Bregman, Peter. "If You Want People to Listen, Stop Talking." HBR.org, May 25, 2015. https://hbr.org/2015/05/if-you -want-people-to-listen-stop-talking.

David, Susan. "Manage a Difficult Conversation with Emotional Intelligence." HBR.org, June 19, 2014. https://hbr .org/2014/06/manage-a-difficult-conversation-with -emotional-intelligence.

David, Susan and Christina Congleton. "Emotional Agility," *Harvard Business Review*, November 2013 (product # R1311L).

DeSteno, David. "The Simplest Way to Build Trust." HBR.org, June 2, 2014. https://hbr.org/2014/06/the-simplest-way -to-build-trust.

Dillon, Karen. *HBR Guide to Office Politics*. Boston: Harvard Business Review Press, 2015.

Goleman, Daniel. "What Makes a Leader?" *Harvard Business Review*, June 1996 (product #R0401H).

Goleman, Daniel, Richard Boyatzis, and Annie McKee. "Primal Leadership: The Hidden Driver of Great Perfor-mance." *Harvard Business Review*, December 2001 (product #R0111C).

Goulston, Mark. "Don't Get Defensive: Communication Tips for the Vigilant." HBR.org, November 15, 2013. https:// hbr.org/2013/11/dont-get-defensive-communication-tips -for-the-vigilant.

Goulston, Mark. "How to Know If You Talk Too Much." HBR .org, June 3, 2015. https://hbr.org/2015/06/how-to-know -if-you-talk-too-much.

Goulston, Mark. "How Well Do You Communicate Dur-ing Conflict?" HBR.org Assessment, March 6, 2015. https://hbr.org/2015/03/assessment-how-well-do-you -communicate-during-conflict-2.

Halvorson, Heidi Grant. *No One Understands You and What to Do about It*. Boston: Harvard Business Review Press, 2015.

Hedges, Kristi. "Five Essential Communication Skills to Catapult Your Career." HBR.org Webinar, Septem-ber 5, 2014. https://hbr.org/2014/09/5-essential -communications-skills-to-catapult-your-career.

Hurley, Robert F. "The Decision to Trust." *Harvard Business Review*, September 2006 (product #R0609B).

Knight, Rebecca. "How to Handle Difficult Conversations at Work." HBR.org, January 9, 2015. https://hbr.org/2015/01/how-to-handle-difficult-conversations-at-work.

Manzoni, Jean-François. "A Better Way to Deliver Bad News." *Harvard Business Review*, September 2002 (product #R0209J).

Tate, Carson. "Differing Work Styles Can Help Team Performance." *Harvard Business Review*, April 3, 2015. https://hbr.org/2015/04/differing-work-styles-can-help-team-performance.

Weeks, Holly. *Failure to Communicate: How Conversations Go Wrong and What You Can Do to Right Them*. Boston: Harvard Business Review Press, 2010.

Wilkins, Muriel Maignan. "Signs You're Being Passive-Aggressive." HBR.org, June 20, 2014. https://hbr.org/2014/06/signs-youre-being-passive-aggressive.

Index

Notes

Notes

Notes

Advice you can quickly read and apply.

Looking for more? Get up to speed fast on the most essential business skills with HBR's 20-Minute Manager Boxed Set. Whether you need a crash course or a brief refresher, this 10-volume collection of concise, practical primers will help you brush up on key management topics.

HBR's 20-Minute Manager Series

Available in paperback or ebook format.

- Creating Business Plans
- Delegating Work
- Difficult Conversations
- Finance Basics
- Getting Work Done
- Giving Effective Feedback
- Innovative Teams
- Leading Virtual Teams

- Managing Projects
- Managing Time
- Managing Up
- Performance Reviews
- Presentations
- Running Meetings
- Running Virtual Meetings
- Virtual Collaboration

HBR.ORG/20MINUTES

Buy for your team, clients, or event.
Visit hbr.org/bulksales for quantity discount rates.

Smart advice and inspiration from a source you trust.

If you enjoyed this book and want more comprehensive guidance on essential professional skills, turn to the HBR Guides Boxed Set. Packed with the practical advice you need to succeed, this seven-volume collection provides smart answers to your most pressing work challenges.

Harvard Business Review Guides

Available in paperback or ebook format. Plus, find downloadable tools and templates to help you get started.

- Better Business Writing
- Building Your Business Case
- Buying a Small Business
- Coaching Employees
- Delivering Effective Feedback
- Finance Basics for Managers
- Getting the Mentoring You Need
- Getting the Right Work Done

- Leading Teams
- Making Every Meeting Matter
- Managing Stress at Work
- Managing Up and Across
- Negotiating
- Office Politics
- Persuasive Presentations
- Project Management